QTR Books
Peekskill, NY
qtr@gmail.com

First Edition, 2018, QTR Books

ISBN-13: 978-1727438079
ISBN-10: 1727438078

Photographs by Walter Rabetz
Book Design by Marilyn Rabetz

Shadows from Unfinished Things

Andrea Barton

Dom Failla

James Finnegan

James Govoni

Marilyn Johnston

Audrey Newell

Walter Rabetz

———————————

Edited by Dom Failla

Photographs by Walter Rabetz

Design by Marilyn Rabetz

INTRODUCTION

The word anthology refers to a collection of literary flowers. Each flower animates, gives soul to a unique perspective that embraces what is profoundly human. In this collection of poems one senses and hears the sound of each poet engaged in bringing to the surface the inner movements to make present their unique experiences.

If one places our ears to these poems, what do we hear? Do we hear and feel the *'gravitational pull toward nothing'*? Do we sense the growing distances and *'subtle changes that enrich the depths of love'*? Can we discern the agonizing decision whether to leave one's family? That is to say, leave the conventional familiar patterns so that we can *'draw hearts,'* around what we love. Perhaps, even to search and find one's unique and fruitful voice.

Yes, the creative process demands that the poet does not hide behind conventions. It demands the courage, to *'unlock and flow'*, to share and eat the *'bread of oblivion'* that cuts through the *'natural order of creation.'* It demands the ever resounding question: *'what do men and women do with their daylight.'*

– Dom Failla

TABLE OF CONTENTS

Dom Failla

11	The Light of the Unseen
12	Poetry Lines
13	Dionysus
14	My Left
15	Buddha
16	God Save Us From the Grammarians
17	Morning
18	Dark Rain
19	Nota Bene
20	It's No Use
21	The Speaking Tree

Andrea Barton

25	This is a Poem About Nothing
26	Philosophy
27	passionately i
28	On Writing Poetry Today
30	Strata
32	Trajectories
34	Unfinished

Marilyn Johnston

39	Walking Eastham's Flats
40	Panda Eyes in the Library
41	Self Memo on Reading
42	Teaching the Angels
44	Flame-Shaped Buddhas
46	Chihuli's Glass

James Finnegan

53	One Windblown
54	Collision of the Sunken City with the Floating World
56	Last Voyage of Palinurus
58	Solzhenitsyn in Cavendish, Vermont
60	Arvo Pärt
62	Giotto's Circle
63	Day Sail
64	Beast and God
66	The Hour of Trucks

TABLE OF CONTENTS

68   Pugnacio
69   Roofs
70   Love Among the Rooms

James Govoni

75   Behind the Panther Moon
76   White Lady
77   Complexes
78   Crocodile
79   Dear Nurse
80   Laying Down the Mulch
81   The Devil is a Metaphysical Taruth
82   Rose Hill
83   Lear-like King
84   The Song of Saint James

Audrey Newell

87   The Jack Pine Has Evolved
88   Sunday Picnic
89   Taking Shape
90   Your Apartment Near North Beach
91   Cowboy Steve
92   I Don't Believe in God
93   (2432)
94   The Fisher King
95   Funk and Precaution / Irregular Journaling
96   If People Were Trees

Walter Rabetz

101   My Shadow
102   Two Men Walking
103   April 8th
104   Your Time
105   Ode to Billy Parker
106   My Special Wonderful Death
107   There But For the Grace of God, Go I
108   OMG! When? How?

All photographs in the book are by Walter Rabetz

DOM FAILLA

DOMINIC FAILLA holds a Ph.D in the Humanities form Florida State University. For many years, he has taught philosophy, religion, and psychology at a private school in Connecticut. He is the author of the *Potemkin Village, The Philosophy of Giambattista Vico,* and a collection of poetry entitled *A Fist Full of Stars.*

The Light of the Unseen

We are made

by the light

of the unseen

No wonder

all the gods die

laughing

along the road of creations.

We remain

orphans of the invisible

whispering

old fairy tales

sin and redemption

around the campfires

of the night.

Poetry Lines

My lines are short,

and shy.

Frequently,

out of breath

No rhymes

no reasons.

Only homeless

images,

playing ghost

behind the masks

of naked words.

Dionysus

I had buried you

under a pine tree

outside

the house of my dreams.

You dark god

of the vineyards

of my childhood memories.

king of the sweet grape

the god

I keep forgetting

in the sanctuary

of my unlived life

.

My Left

My left
over my right foot
   ready for the crucifixion,
    ready for the nails
     that immobilize
  what I know
and dare not love,
   and what I love
  and dare not to know.
This is the painful
   Sleep.

Buddha

What do you hold
In your empty cup
of simplicity?
The unborn sky,
dancing horizons
knocking
at the door of joy,
holy rain
falling on the face
of silent stones,
dark songs
dazzling the soul
of compassion.
What do you hold
in your cup
full of small miracles?

"God Save Us From the Grammarians"
Nietzsche

Don't use the "I"

use the third person "He"

as if I didn't have difficulty

with the first.

Acquire distance

objectivity

as if my body

Smelled of life.

Make certain you include

The Holy Trinity - -

opening paragraph

mutilated body

the inexorable conclusion.

And, for God' sake,

above all,

don't forget

your footnotes,

don't plagarize

the Living and the dead.

Morning

Early morning

waiting

for the white eyes

of winter show.

Wondering,

Can boundary stones

ever be re-arranged?

Can graves

and green ghosts,

marching to the beat

of the martial music's lost reasons,

ever be awakened?

What else can one do

With the bleeding morning

of darkness.

Dark Rain

For the first time
I look
the dark rain
in the eye.
It's the only way
to see a new
morning rising
from the breath
of silence
from the clean
hands of joy.

Nota Bene

What do the dead
want to see?
What do they underline
with their eyes closed,
and small ears
close to the grave
Their breathless joy
is to taste
the invisible wind
and navigate
the enriching arms
of the restless
light of creation.

It's No Use

re-telling the story
the page is missing
the lines do not exist.
the depth is a white phantom.
So, gently whisper
night stars into your passing words
no one owns
the sacramental host
of the days and nights
of your life.

The Speaking Tree

I speak because the spirit
robs me of joy and life if I do not speak.

C.G. Jung

Yes, I speak

The language of the enemy!

Afraid

to give myself away.

I curl my tongue

just like you

my tormentor

and liberator.

Thanks to you

I have found my voice

under

the speaking tree.

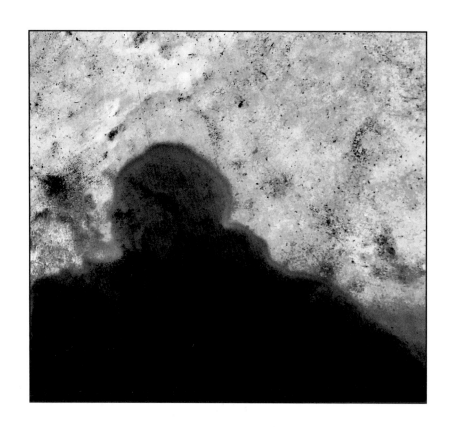

ANDREA BARTON

ANDREA BARTON is a mother, a daughter, a poet, and a teacher, in that order. Her work has appeared in publications such as The Labletter, The Cleave Webzine, Broken Publications, (a journal of domestic violence), Haiku Journal #42, The *2016 Bards Against Hunger Anthology*, and frequently in her local newspaper. From 2009-2012 she ran a Monday night poetry series at *Cafemantic* in Willimantic, CT. She has taught Creative Writing, American Lit, and Communications at RHAM High School in Hebron, CT for over 20 years, but her greatest achievement to date is her 14 year old daughter, who is still bright and lovely and sparkly, despite her adolescence. Andrea, her daughter, and their fluffy dog, Jack, live on 4 acres of ticks and spiders and yard work in Glastonbury, CT.

This is a Poem About Nothing

She

is the last stanza

in this house,

her shoulders slumped

and sagging,

like the roof giving up

with its sad smile, a sigh, no more.

Everything around her is sinking

lower

and

lower,

and she's lighting another cigarette,

watching the smoke curl

across a blade of sun that fell in

to the window by accident.

It's a love song

turning into

an elegy.

The weight of her life

is what's pressing her,

the mass of nothing,

the way nothing traps you

when it's all you have.

Philosophy

I love
what stained glass
does to a strand of sun.
It makes philosophy
out of the practical.

passionately
i

am the

universe

airless vast void

i am the galax

y tilted elliptic

al swirl matter known and un

known i am the blue-tinted plan

et wobbling as i go i am the

land growing dying rising falling a

way i am the buildings wood stone concrete i

am a letter to the editor of hand-tossed

newspapers that will disintegrate i am the sum

of all that has passed plus the subtraction of all i have

lost i am a mass of warm red cells traveling in an end

less circuit together madly sadly passionately i

On Writing Poetry Today

There was
no poem today,
no knock-knock, knock
like a neighbor's call
on the metaphorical door.
I made coffee
by myself
and didn't even look
for a pen
or paper
because what need did I have,
sitting there alone
this morning,
with not a poem in the world
on my mind?
And yet
the hands of the clock
moved purposefully forward
stepbystep
by step by
step
by

step

by

step

as I worked my way through the
grocery store flyer.

I did think of a recipe-
(chicken divan)
but that isn't a poem
even if I put the white wine in it,
so I made chili instead.

There is very little poetry
in the mop bucket,
or laundry,
or in the clean sheets,
I discovered,
but I wasn't looking.

Maybe tomorrow a poem will come
to the metaphorical door.
If I'm home,
I'll answer it.

Strata

Everything depends on a layer,
like sunflowers depend on topsoil
like violet, indigo, blue, green
yellow, and orange depend
on the red depending on rain.
The way the top note of a chord
expects the other notes to hold it up,
like how next year
depends on this year
being wrapped around last year
on this tree.

Everything depends on a layer
like the weight of strata
compressing a sunset:
stratosphere,
troposphere,
clouds,
then everything
depends on pink.
Like a canyon depends on the mesa
to give up

its layers to the river,

like grief depends on the presence

then the absence

then the forever,

like bones depend on wind.

Everything depends on a layer.

Like earth depends on a strip

of air

to protect it from hurtling matter

like my heart depends

on skin

to protect it

from the serrated side

of your love.

Trajectories

We are swimming in Sedona after sunset
and through a gap in the trees
I can see Jupiter and Venus
hanging companionably on the horizon
looking back at us like a wistful old couple.
Macy paddles close to me
and as soon as I can touch the bottom,
wraps her arms around my neck
wanting me to carry her around the water,
planting fat smacking kisses on my cheeks.
Tomorrow will be momentous,
but we don't know it yet.
We laugh while we race and play,
splashing under the just-waking-up stars.
Always she hovers around me,
my own satellite, my own Calisto.

I look up to the pair of planets
framed in the space between those two trees,
my eleven year old child playing baby in my arms.
Tomorrow and the next day and the next day

they will be driven apart by a few degrees,

a few more degrees more degrees more degrees

the distance-

it grows,

each planet in its own orbit, helpless

in its trajectory.

They will meet again, next year,

but so much on our planet will be different then:

the coming, the going,

the change that never changes.

None of us

can go back.

Unfinished

The cat is curled
in her bed like
a comma;

I am waiting
for a storm
to arrive.

It is dark
out there
though moonlight

is bouncing off
snow in the clouds
that hasn't yet

begun to fall
so there is more
than my reflection

to look at,
more than the first
layer of woods

to see into.
The sound of snow
almost - not - quite -

falling at night
is draped over my head
like a hijab.

I think about
shadows and
unfinished things.

MARILYN JOHNSTON

MARILYN JOHNSTON'S poetry has received six Pushcart nominations. Her first chapbook, *Against Disappearance* was published as Finalist for the 2001 Poetry of Redgreene Press, Pittsburg. She is the author of two full collections: *Silk First Songs* (2008) and *Weight of the Angel* (2009) published by Antrim House Books. Her poetry has appeared in numerous journals, *South Carolina Review, Worcester Review. Rattle Poet Lore.* She co-founded and directed for twenty years the ongoing Wintonbury Poetry Reading Series in the Bloomfield Libraries. She retired from the library in 2017.

Walking Eastham's Flats

Love lies with the low eaves of Beach Rose Cottage--
we untangle the ribbons of a windsock
color by color with the wind's help, gently
undo the knots in the long fluttering currents,
then let the separate ribbons fly
red from blue, yellow from green,
purple from orange. Bound as they are
on the white cuff etched with a red anchor,
light lifts them. Every day we eat bread's
oblivion. Today we walk
the seabed where the blue bay has receded
showing ribbons of sand imprinted by
opportunist gulls, their feet and ours
sinking in with weight, prints
the returning tide covers.
One can be happy with the elemental.
It seems to ask less and less,
the hands holding, then in the infinite expanse,
broken apart, finding, regripping, once again
walking Eastham's flats, after all the breaking
of wishbones, in the bodies we have.

Panda Eyes in the Library

Dominic enters, wearing his panda hat:
white knit skull topped with black bear ears,
two black-rimmed eye-holes pulled up on his brow.
I'm going to have call you four eyes, I say.

No, you can't. He yanks
panda eyes over his glasses.
He comes here to escape the world.

We two are on a plane of discourse we share instantly
no one else aboard
and always the terrorists trying to kick us off.

Come to the open mic!
Don't you write? And he shows me
a poem…in his scribbled hand about dashing fate.

It's strong. Who writes about fate anymore?
Nobody, that's who, I say. "You mean, " young,
he launches into his best youth imitation…"it's all:
Bee bop to the hip hop to the flash dash
slap blab, fist to the crisp into the ocean of emotion?…"

and we laugh. He looks at me
from out of his panda eyes, then
shakes my hand, walks out the backdoor,
descending again to the far east forest he hides in.

Self-Memo on Reading

Ciardi, but I would add also, of love--
when you say "Every discovery
of true correspondence is an act
of reason and of instruction." Love
saves you from yourself I think
most, and from the sharp
spears of "superiority" brandished by others.
To use it, mental acuity--
that clumsy spear on your forehead
helps you survive
but never use it against anyone.
Let drain all those red-faced moments
and re-employ the saved blood
back for strength
needed to augment papier-mâché
age. Keep writing in that
soul-filled boom.
Someone needs words
in this way, perhaps everyone does.

Teaching the Angels .

We order soup, don't eat it, and pay
the entire luncheon tab for others
then try to collect in understanding.
Bear the most terrestrial of sodden
wings in poisonous updrafts. Plead
with anger, fend with love.
This is the human way:
to look straight, eye to eye,
with ardor, then be wounded on the other side
in simultaneous gloom. If you like
your empyrean unmixed,
don't try this at home. For us,
things are weighted and transcendent.
They're neither one nor the other alone.
Here, we must watch high school rings
age on skin-draped bones. Watch roles
shift and move in time like forward-moving
frogs who never hop
backwards, but carry past and present

paths into a future strangeness.
Ardent striving in endless practice's
no guarantee we improve at anything
and the meager hope of souls grasped
for warmth and security
can, in an eye blink, be torn from us.
We start out awed and cowed,
small in a phantasmagoric landscape
that shrinks in time to a chessboard
barren and cold because in the end
though we come replete with bravura
"We're going to change Aging!"
we are changed.
My suggestion: stay
angels, stay apart. Forestall curiosity
about our realm. Stay,
drift as you've always done. Don't
delve. Don't venture.
Don't learn.

Flame–Shaped Buddha

penetrates the entangled brain

last night's insomnia
head follicles kept me awake
grown wild whipped
beach-thick slapped with gel:

No one could get a comb through this

Living in a cold dark wood

It takes so little to tip
the staid life to the other side
as though to sit and dream
of a twenty-first-century unmarred
by violence

is to dream of forty underwater black cats
curled contentedly on a pool floor
undisturbed chess pieces on a field of white
seen through water…

Oh the body is still passably slim if

going toward skeletal-fleshy

but you really can't

suffer being young anymore

though I tell you: no one can be

exclusively

old.

Living

seven ages insures repetition of

unfamiliar un-sureness

and a flame-shaped Buddha still sits

as your guide as the snow falls.

Chihuli's Glass

Spears shoot athwart the Arno River
on the strength of his propelling arm.
A chandelier swings multi-breasted blue
Artemis slung off a bridge
over the Grand Canal. The form is
emptiness won by a pressure of breath,
opened by fire. Squeezed, condensed, cut.
Hardened, molten, handled by asbestos gloves.
Let it twirl in the sun off its
metal racks…Like a poem by Williams,
intricate, gleaming, clean
as green glass blown free-hand
in the first half of the twentieth century
sealed by his eclipsed breath
in shards still shining between walls
the back wings /of the/ hospital.
He said: unlock and flow…be nothing.
I'm afraid to flow. Afraid to let
go, and what's the first thing
they ever thought to make
of fluid glass? Containers.
…In pieces, they say time

can never break down glass

unless it's shattered. Glittering

purple, gilt-leaf bottles

of some ancient nameless Egyptian

lady-in-waiting stand elegantly

intact after two millennia. Kings

fear natural flow obliterates the rational

order. So, pyramids--

not perfume bottles, yet

a maker embodies eternal laws

of hydrodynamics, learns to breathe

in stops, twists, step changes

in direction, shape--

swing the blob on the end of a long hollow pole

in a continuous free-flow dance

so that expanding glass becomes the form

of his every living motion--

in the back-breaking work

by the raging furnace. In creation, timing

and temperature are everything. Fatigue,

and impatient plying weakens glass

along its inner lines of stress

fracturing webs of hairline cracks,

cooling. Chihuly shows
the molten mass must be gathered up
glowing, worked and transformed
if transformed at all
            in its burning moment,
that's all we have…

                        Dreams
call us into the velvet
dark, shimmering under high intensity
bulbs. Polished glass like water caught
in the shapes of open shells. Arrogant,
foolhardy, fragile, unhandlable
beauty begging to be stroked and shattered
while we walk all the way around
each lonely pedestal, hushed,
worshipping.

JAMES FINNEGAN

JAMES FINNEGAN'S poems have appeared in *Ploughshares*, *Poetry Northwest*, *The Southern Review*, *The Virginia Quarterly Review*, as well as in the anthologies *Good Poems: American and Laureates of Connecticut*. With Dennis Barone he edited *Visiting Wallace: Poems Inspired by the Life and Work of Wallace Stevens*. He is the president of the F*riends & Enemies of Wallace Stevens* (stevenspoetry.org). His aphoristic ars poetica can be found at the blog ursprache (https://ursprache.blogspot.com).

One Windblown

Leaving again, leaving behind my slowly dying mother,
driving to the airport on an early May morning.
My rental car headed toward that great control tower
looming at the horizon, jets from everywhichwhere
juggled in the pure blue sky. The air is filled with
cottonwood seeds, released to the whims of the wind.
They rise and fall in the push-pull of highway traffic.
I'll come back from time to time if she lives on.
I'll come back certainly for her funeral. I'm that tiny
dark seed embedded in a tuft of cottonwood fluff,
I am windblown. The one in my family who went away
and never returned. I keep telling myself she knows me,
and she does in the moment the pupils of her eyes
fix upon me. Each aperture about the size of a seed.
She blinks, and I'm gone, once again given to the wind.

Collision of the Sunken City
with the Floating World

To be double-blessed like birds
of a floating world. We still sail
by tongue or leaf or low-slung moon,
sometimes. There are days when
our roofs turn as sails against red sunsets
going deep pink with the windblown clouds.
There will soon be an evening star cum planet,
one of those called wanderers. Once the sky
was enough, ethereal yet sustenance.
Now it holds less stars. Light pollution
they say. I often forget and use less

                              when I mean fewer,
or fewer when I want to say yes. Less or fewer,
doesn't seem that those times of flight,
of song, of high-held breath in love,
are not so many so high so much
so pure as they once were? Meaning
I don't want to be after, don't want to be late,
nor lapse to past, later or last things.

When I look down, and more and more
that is where my eyes are relegated, I see
there's mud on my shoes. Reminder
that I've come to the sunken city.
A place built from concrete and regret.
Glass windows that can't be broken but
won't reflect either. Rather than wipe them,
I'll slip my shoes off at the backdoor, ascend
the first stairway that presents itself.

Originally published in Laureates of Connecticut: An Anthology of Contemporary Poetry (Grayson Books, 2017)

Last Night of the Palinurus

Palinurus, you placed too much trust in the sky and the ocean's calm.
Now you lie naked and dead on the sands of an unknown shore.

Aeneas, know this, I never sailed for you.

I was your helmsman, I was your true

guide through many a strait and scrape,

but to find home was my end and escape.

While you pursued, hungered for the fray,

I sought the safer course, another way.

Those cloud-ships forever and ever flee

to what sky's edge, flotilla of futility?

I tried all my life to avoid intrigue, desires,

flesh-greed from which a body never tires.

You were my master, and I watched as you

rushed to arms, into the arms of Dido too.

There was much to admire in you, Aeneas,

but lead and I follow was all that made an *us.*

When the waters heaved and the winds flew,

the heart was the only chart you knew.

You said your strength would be my balm,

yet I knew no sense of peace or calm

in all my days owned and bound to you.

So one last storm will see me through,

our fates sealed uneasily in heavy rips.

When a ship goes over, and the hand slips

from the tiller, the rudder will rise like a fin

for a moment in the waves, like a dolphin.

There will always be a wind over the sea,

a voice in the air calling out orders to me.

I hear when my body washed ashore

it came so with the grace of a swimmer.

Solzhenitsyn in Cavendish, Vermont

Driving through those small towns of Vermont,
feeling myself a stranger, I sometimes think of him.
How odd it must have been
after the burning cities, after the Boss's purges,
after years spent in a gulag, I think of Comrade S
walking the roads of Cavendish. Perhaps
one's whole life is exile from the womb,
but why and whereby is he here. Stepping through snow
up to his shins, at least that's familiar.
Nearly twenty years spent in Vermont, companionable
landscape, yet he is alien without their language.
Someone waves from a red pickup, he waves back.
Watching the blue glow of TV's burn inside their homes,
imagining them gathered round these faux hearths
in their living rooms. Ease and amnesia being sold
during commercial breaks. Why not go back to Russia
now that the wall has fallen, but go back in spring.
Spring is the earth's reward for living another year.
In the old USSR he's a hero, but his honor ran out on one
of those marches through the Prussian nights.

Every flag impersonates a wing, wants to be
free even as it hooks to its stanchion.
The wind whips it, and the clasps make a jangly music
against the metal pole. In time the wind tatters
the flag to strips and wisps that fly off.
Even government of and for and by the people fails,
because *of* the people. We are the part that breaks
in the ideal machine. You can hear when a bolthead shears off,
bangs around inside the tractor's engine cover,
doing more damage. The farm animals stop, their heads
tilt up unable to understand human shouts, curses,
then they move slowly toward the comfort of fences,
their borders. Hawks Mountain black against the early sun.
Mister S, is what they call him at the grocery. He knows
that history is but a matter of better and worse days.

.

Arvo Pärt

A man opened the heavy church door, stuck
his head out saying, *Are you coming in? The concert
is about to start*. We hadn't planned on this.
Answering with the affirmative nod between lovers
who must forever fall unexpectedly into the lap of chance.
When we entered we saw a small chamber group

arranged in front of the altar. Counting us there were less
than ten in the audience. You feel you're important
to the proceedings when you're one of so few. Still one
had to feel a little sorry for the musicians, who must practice
their craft long hours, often alone, and now on the date
of their performance, this paltry number here to hear.

In the nave's tall windows branches of trees wavered.
You could see but the tips of buds before leaves.
We had almost stopped believing in spring
after that hard winter. Maybe the man who opened
that door was Arvo Pärt. Because forever hence,
the Estonian composer's *Spiegel im Spiegel*,

Passacaglia, Fratres, Da Pacem Domine, not the titles
but his music will be part of our memory,
those strange modern strains of sacred music.
The violins, one viola, single standing cello, plus grand piano.
If there is a God, he must bless those chamber players
who played as though a thousand people filled the hall.

Only an hour or so before we'd been making love
in the late afternoon. And now to be given this extra time
together, an event that should never have been.
We hold hands as we listen to the final movement
while the light fades from those tall windows, the world outside
dims again, a beauty almost missed, sans music.

Giotto's Circle

As Vasari's story goes, Giotto's signature
was a single perfect circle. Drawn in red, freehand
and quickly, almost casually to send a message to a Pope.
A circle that rippled over the seas...around the earth,
and widens still.

Confidence in one's talent and facility
is a funny thing. It can come and go. By now
you must know that art is that circle. One that both
widens and tightens. It lets us in, but then as easily
it holds us out.

Sometimes we are inside the bait ball of small fish
that larger predatory fish keep reforming
and perfecting with their teeth. Sometimes the wobble
of a far planet means a dead star disturbs its orbit,
slowly reels it in.

It took a long time to realize your gift would never
be Giotto's. That whatever circle you might draw
would be more like a tire that needed air. One hears
it throb and moan over miles of pavement, but
O, it rolls on.

Day Sail

In memory of BGM

Those sails out there on the horizon,
gray-white, flaring up in the late day sun.
I think of you out there, at the end of a day sail.

That white sheet is beautiful and pure
against the wind, far away from arguing
the finer points of the four corners of a contract.

When the powerboat fades in the distance,
it's only the sail's snap you hear, and that tink-tink
of the stays, which is as much of silence as one gets.

So allow me today, on this beautiful day for sailing,
to think of those sails as souls plying this earth,
searching for a steady wind or a fair harbor.

And allow me to remember the man I knew.
We never doubted your sense of direction,
we who were left standing dockside waiting.

The fog is beginning to build on the sound tonight.
One by one the stars will be extinguished. Turn her,
turn her before the lights from the shore go too.

Beast and God

He who is unable to live in society, or who has no
need because he is sufficient for himself, must be
either a beast or a god: he is no part of a state.
                              — Aristotle, Politics, Book I

Self-exiled inside my own life,
at times I believe I'm both beast
and god because I have no needs
and need of none. Alone
I'll answer no phone, ignore
any knock at the door. A face
pressed to the front window,
will see nothing but an empty chair,
a book hanging open over the arm
under a cone of lamplight.

I'm up on the roof, hanging over
the cornice, trading grimaces with
the gargoyles. Listening to the music
of insects as they fill the air.
And naming the stars before their light
penetrates the atmosphere of this earth.

Why don't you write me a note
that I won't answer. People keep
trying to save, try to welcome me
into their company, save a pew
for me in church. But no flock welcomes
a falcon when it dives into their midst.

My mother was yeti, screeching
up on a mountain mornings as sunlight
reached the treeline. My father carried
his own coffin like a canoe down
to the river at dusk. True, I was pulled up
by the roots at an early age. Opening
cans with my teeth when I was hungry.
But I am not beset, nor lonely.
Don't mistake your lack for mine.
I have a city state, a solar plexus
of avenues, lodged under my sternum.

The Hour of Trucks

Sometime after midnight
when the trucks own
the highway and all the houses
in the hills have given back
what light they have
to the few stars scattered
above the horizon, inside
their cabs little galaxies
of dials and gauges mark
the speed and fuel level,
while outside the headlights
and tail-lights stream and diverge
without worry of speed traps
or weigh stations, and the minds
of drivers go blank, gray out
like the dimly lit asphalt
that runs forever ahead of them,
till it's hard to recall
what it is they're hauling,
only destinations are known,
with the names of cities painted

In large white letters looming

on overhead signs, so there's no

excuse to miss an exit, and if there

is a place called home it's faraway now,

in a wash of litter and exhaust

the apparitions of loved ones

kicked up and dissipating

in the air swirling

behind their trailers,

as they pull their loads

toward morning.

Pugnacio

At the weigh-in I knew I'd lost the fight.
I'd come down to make weight, Pugnacio
was moving up a class. He's been fighting
up all his life. He marked me as a tourist.
I've always had the body of an athlete,
never had to try too hard to exceed.
I haven't had a thing to drink since my training
started, but still it feels like I have a buzz on.
That's the brain cells sizzling after a right
cross to the temple, the one I didn't see
that fells me. And I won't see him either,
but I'll know he's there, Pugnacio standing
over me, watching as I try to get one knee
under my body. Waiting to see if I rise from
the canvas, open my eyes to meet his stare.

Roofs

If you look down over the valley or up
along the hillsides, you'll see all the roofs.
These are the unread books of the world,
forever splayed face down where they
were laid half-read unto eternity, fire or tear down,
their roofline spines too thin to hold a title
or family name. But underneath each one,
inside each one, a slow novel unfolds
over many years. People love, people die,
days spent in struggle and those that pass
with unnoticed ease, all the little and large events,
walls, ceilings, floors, pages written with their lives.
Under one of these roofs I live. I can't start
the story over from here, and I don't know
what happens next in the book I call home.

Love Among the Rooms

Often we have met in galleries
and museums. Sometimes walking
the walls together, other times apart.

I'll catch your figure from across a room,
at times your face is close to a painting,
inspecting the brushstrokes,

other times, you're standing back, gazing
powerfully. And when I come near,
you offer an insight about space or color.

Rooms that both separate and join us.
I turn a corner, and when you fix me in your eyes,
let me be your art, or else over my shoulder
be there an important work to behold.

JAMES GOVONI

JIM GOVONI is a Licensed Professional Counselor with graduate degrees in art education and counseling. Jim's long standing interest in art, yoga and Jungian Psychology led him into poetry as a way to bring meaning into the second half of life. He is a member of The Meeting House Poets. The Meeting House Poets is a group of Connecticut poetry writers and performers. Jim's work has appeared in the *Wising Up Press Anthology: Creativity and Constraint* (2015) and *BEATITUDE* – 10th Anniversary Edition (2018).

Behind The Panther Moon

I am the water bird

that flees through the deserted sky

tugged from below by an uncertain sea

how fair or foul this Charon be

breaking toward a cameo moon

a panther faced diorama

veils a grey city

overrun by children

in black uniforms

playing wildly

unfazed and alone

sooty and grim

I arrive

the outcast, guest or prophet

to an orphaned world

White Lady

My life's vessel wallows
your expanding face swallows
all I love into the eternal sea.
Goddess death
I trace your shadow with my finger of blame
beckon to reckon
with your unintentional intention
to wipe my slate clean.

Complexes

What I cannot see

grabs me

shakes me

smittens me

angers me

overwhelmed

touched

      by random buttons

pushed

      by that figure behind the curtain

a god I cannot see

do not want to see

in me.

          © J. Govoni. December 2014

Crocodile

How did it become my fate
to find a crocodile as my soulmate.
Cold blooded reptile who visits in dream
whether I like it or not he affects my esteem.
At times he is friendly and I hold no fear.
Other times his motives remain unclear.
Why is he here and wanting to play?
Rhyme or reason says keep him at bay.
I find this creature becoming a treasure
beyond feared jaws and savage leather.
But, first I must make him my keeper
this allows me in turn to go even deeper
by accepting him as a piece of my soul
where hubris or madness are not in control.
There I ask him, what are you in me?
Then our dialogue leads to what I don't see.
From the beast who is so timeless and strange
I learn wisdom is earned by challenge and change.
For me this is seeing what I become
then accepting-rejecting turning into clay
reshaping-rebuilding what I had cast away.

© J. Govoni, February 2018

Dear Nurse

Nightingale of indistinct gender

Unconcerned if one loved or used you

Always a primitive pendent hung on your chest

Worn like a shaman from another time

Your talk of fossils and stars

Is where your kind mana drew its source

In endless passion to serve others

Devoid of hubris

You cared only about caring

Dear nurse

We that are left behind sigh

And smile that's just like you

To leave us this way

As your ashes

Fade into the rhythm of the waves

© J. Govoni, August, 2014

Laying Down the Mulch

Smoothing over

covering up

rather than digging deep

choosing what I hope will grow

opening to the light

making bright

showcasing

what is mine

what I love

my flowers

my joy.

As I smother what yet is born

never able to stop the weeds

even by denying the sun

for the moon does not care

it gives light to the dark

nurturing shadows in earthen wombs

forming no graves for unborn truths

allowing reality

to break through earth's soft skin

roughing up the dreams of this fool

who decorates with a sweet cedar face

-laying down the mulch.

The Devil is a Metaphysical Truth

(for Leonard C)

Whore of habit
mistress of delight
you keep me warm
throughout the night.

I hold on to you
my playful friend
while you sacrifice
me to bitter end.

Will I ever learn
to struggle free
satisfying you
pleasuring me?

Whore of habit
mistress of delight
I don't know why
this holy fight?

You are my love
the devil I spite
but I can't release
our sacred rite

Rose Hill

(A Haibun)

As I pass its baroque gates, the now bright air remains dampened by whiffs of swelling worms and sweet sour mulch. Greetings to those who journey out of love or sentiment, commitment or obligation. I follow the one way road that winds its double helix path through a mise en scene of rolling lawns, pinched perfect trees and pastel shrubs. Here, robbed of their playground, neurotic squirrels shift frantically to and fro as bored cement saints gaze over a sea of divots arranged in tight military order. Each notch plugged by a bronze nameplate. Guest tags in this prepaid community that has no windows, no locks, no fears. All here equal, all here secure. Mowers routinely buzz, trimmers whine their undulating rhythms as the be-bop of bordering traffic no longer jangles the nerves of its residents. In their clay mangers, resting on beds of silk and steel, Mom and Dad in quiet decay look up in silence.

God's pastoral face
Chuckling at all vanities
Universe unmoved

Lear-like King

I wander in dreams
into a half-remembered life
thirsting for the milk of the familiar
pining for lost times
Dionysian times
seeking the holiness
the comforting hollowness
of once sacred places.
This Lear-like King
desiring to be
a bewildered and raptured boy
dancing now in slumber
with his fading soul.

The Song of Saint James
...unsettled notes from a dream

Alone with the masses on the Boardwalk of Flaws
overstuffed hucksters bark with snap-trap jaws
to prophet-less fish from a crowded sea
these carnival men roam freer than me.

You! Sir! Have you ever heard !

Fat barker says with baited look:

The Song of St. James
a golden hymn from
The Great American Song Book.

I retort:
My name is James
why to me do you turn?
Am I in the song you speak
and what may I learn?

Don't give me some jingle
like a George M. Cohen tune
that sends praises to a fucking flag
or pines for love under a harvest moon.

Carnival man begins to shift and sway
dodging me on what to say.

I go on:
       Sing me a ballad of the fears
       I'm afraid to know
       hiding in the conventions
       I need to let go
       so I may live my true hymn
       beside the redemptions
       beside the strife
       making up the bible that is my life.

Carnival man looks to the ground.
He grunts but makes no other sound

To his lack of response I say:

       Carnival man, Carnival man
       your trap remains shut
       but your actions are clear
       I see, I see
       the truth of the matter
       rests only with me.

AUDREY NEWELL

AUDREY NEWELL is an adventurous and creative young writer and photographer, currently living in South Africa. As a student at the University of Vermont, she studied poetry under Major Jackson, during which, she found her "storytelling voice". In January 2019, she will return to UVM to complete her degree in Creative Writing, and Global Studies.

The Jack Pine Has Evolved

to withstand fire
    after fire
        careless campfire cigarette flames
        lightning dry September flames
        dead-leaf birch-bark pine-needle flames until
one fire
    so hot
pine resin drips like blood
        and pine cones burst
          and the tree
            burns to the
              ground.

I could never love you like that.

Sunday Picnic / Minigowan Island

Thin, and blonde,
       and younger then,
my mother made lists on yellow lined paper:
three skinned knees, sixteen stubbed
toes, blood, and dirt, and mud, dripping down shins,
I made red handprints on the rocks around me
while she began to explain the importance of hygiene,
but ended up complaining that I was giving her wrinkles
and she was making lists,
weighed down by line after line, letters pushed in deep
and I see the whites of her knuckles
as she records every scratch
and bump and four leeches and two tick bites
in two notebooks, for brother and me,
no list for her or dad yet,
for doctors words that leave cuts like fingernails in flesh,
or the selection of medications lining our kitchen table
and every few minutes, she adjusts the leather purse strap
wearing into her shoulder
as she carries the weight of two yellow notebooks,
       of first aid kits.

Taking Shape

Some days he sculpts long swooping
        curves, like sipping
                smoke. He mimics slow strokes,
slicing away thin wood shavings
        like shedding layers, like letting
                go. Some days he
cuts right
        angles
                leaving deep,
narrow channels
        like words you can't take back,
                like a man who doesn't know
that mahogany cuts
        like butter if you lean into it
                just right.
Some days take familiar shape,
        a woman standing with arms folded,
                a salmon, jumping,
two birds meeting, beak
        to beak.

Your Apartment near North Beach

I remember you brought damp matches

But I didn't mind

And it was raining anyways

And you told me a story

About the time you pierced your ear

With a fishhook,

      In Alaska

And I remember, it was almost November

And you never got the fire started

But my lips weren't shaking

Until the third flight of stairs

When I saw the map on your bedroom wall

And it took me four whole seconds

To trace my finger

      From one coast to another

And I asked you if you ever miss home

But you didn't believe in staying in one place

And I remember when you kissed me,

      You always tasted like somewhere else

Cowboy Steve

Your small town, overall, cut off t-shirt

Tree-trunk arms have hugged me before

The last time I saw you, you called me "kiddo"

But last night when I waved hello, you didn't remember my name

And I could feel your one missing finger

On the small of my back, while you insisted I try all types of bourbon

And I wanted to ask you

"man, what do you do in the daylight?"

my family bought corn from your farm stand for thirteen years

before I learned to draw hearts around names and I thought it was so dreamy

that you loved to bake zucchini bread

and cage fight

and last night you asked why you'd never seen me before, said you wouldn't forget that smile

And I wanted to ask you

"man, what do you do in the daylight?"

You said your favorite band is Godsmack, and being a writer sounds like a waste

of time. You called my friend "Glasses" after she said "Maddy" three times,

then four, and you asked me

if I was scared

And I wanted to ask you

"man, what do you do in the daylight?"

I don't believe in (God)

but I believe in kisses like airport arrival gates.
but I believe in crying for road kill like kids on the news.
but I believe in growing up like blasting through yellow lights.
but I believe in feeling too much like overwatering.
but I believe in depression like riverbed erosion.
but I believe in moving on like a rock in your shoe.
but I believe in small talk like riding a bike with no chain.
but I believe in worship, but I believe in worship,
but I believe in worship.

(2432)

We used	Rent's due	You are
to joke about	sister's in town	needed here, you
things like this,	next Tuesday;	are needed
like death.	don't go.	here, you.

The Fisher King

There's a four-minute window to pull,

not rip,

three barbed hooks shining

next to dull swamp scales.

My thumb rests in the gap between rows of teeth

and thick leather lips;

blood runs down the seam of my pants

and pools with the gasoline in the stern, behind me.

Her body begins to slow,

thrashing once, slitting the skin

between my thumb and pointer finger

and I avoid her too dark eyes as I relieve the last hook

before sinking her body back into murky depths.

For a moment, she lingers.

One fin, turned up towards the gunnels

where I rest my bleeding palm

and I wonder how close she was to dying;

I wonder if she knew.

Funk and Precaution / Irregular Journaling

I made a list of eleven different Hendrix songs, missed you eleven different ways, like if I filled pages with empty words, if I traced those letters just long enough. In June I didn't have anyone to miss so I made a list titled "Affirmations" but all it says is 'And I'm lonely. And I'm lonely. And I'm lonely.

And – '

I am not brave.

If people were trees

maybe my best friend could love herself. Or empty
words could mean something like oxygen, and that smell
you smell when new saplings
       shoot through snow in spring.
Could you imagine? The crunchy granola hippies, chaining themselves
to grandma and grandpa,
"don't cut them down
they are history, they are (significant)."
Standing in old growth, moss so smooth, unshaven,
      (pointing)   that one is leaning   that one drops crab apples   that one
fell over in a storm.
Which one is prettiest?
How do you   choose?

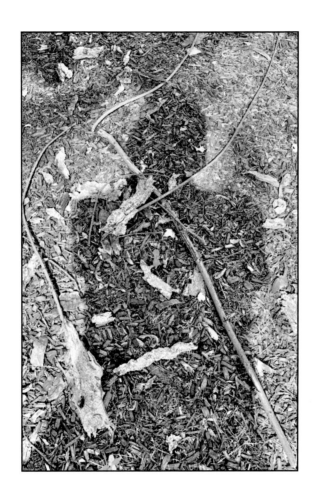

WALTER RABETZ

WALTER RABETZ holds an MFA in Photography from the Rhode Island School of Design. All of the images included in this book are from his *Shadows* series. He was the Chairman of the Art Department at The Loomis Chaffee School for four decades. He is an exhibiting artist and author of more than a dozen books of his work including *The Bear Mountain Bridge, The Jewel of the Hudson; Beauty at the Margins; Manhattan Grit; Home Room; Old Friends; Ocean's Handwriting* among others. He co-authored *A Fistfull of Stars* with Dominic Failla. All of these titles, and more, are available online at Amazon.com.

My Shadow

At some point
　　　　I shall not be
That is of course
　　　　Not up to me

What should be done
　　　　For memory
To leave a trace
　　　　Of life's history

From birth to death
　　　　Life's magic glow
Moves quickly
　　　　With its ebb and flow

The evidence herein is clear
　　　　When I cast this shadow

　　　　　　I stood here.

Two Men Walking

Two men walking:

Two men talking
    Walking . . . talking
        Walking . . . talking
            Laughing . . .talking

One says:

Life is too short

Two men walking
    Not talking
        Thinking . . .walking
            Silent . . . walking

Other says:

Not too short
    Not too long
        It is what it is . . . just right
            It is what it is . . . just right

Walking thinking
    Silent . . .walking
        Silent . . .walking

Are you happy?

Walking . . . not talking
    Thinking . . . not talking
        Sometimes happy . . . sometimes sad
            Sometimes happy . . . Sometimes sad

Just grateful

Grateful for what?

    Grateful to walk
    Grateful to talk
    Grateful to think
    Grateful to laugh

April 8th

It is through tears

      I find myself.

Freeing me from

      Confusion.

The present

      Slowly growing.

The future

      Brightening,

Tears, my kind

      Stepping-stones.

Out of the dark river

      Of my past.

Your Time

There is little time
　　　　　　for regrets,
There is little time
　　　　　　for forgiveness,
There is little time,
　　　　　　for thanks,
There is little time
　　　　　　for amends.

Life is short.

　　　How are you going to use your time?

Ode: To Billy Parker

BILLY COLLINS	gave me poetry
BILLY JOEL	gave me music
BILLY CRYSTAL	gave me comedy
BILLY WILDER	gave me movies
BILLY GRAHAM	gave me preaching
BILLY THE KID	gave me westerns
BILLIE HOLIDAY	gave me the blues
BILLY MARTIN	gave me baseball
BILLIE JEAN KING	gave me women's equality

BILLY PARKER

gave me

FRIENDSHIP

My Special Wonderful Death

The day I was born death joined me.
We bonded in utero and emerged together for life's journey.

We have been together ever since. I do not go or do anything without him.
He is always at my side.

He wants me to be happy, healthy, productive and positive.
Since, he is my private unique death he will cease to be when I cease to be.

"How cool is that?"

We will leave life's magic glow the way we entered – together!
He will do everything to keep me going.

Healthy, happy, productive; anything that needs to be done; a true buddy and dear friend.

I am grateful to have him beside me for life's spectacular blesséd ride.
We are not fearful of the end.

There, but for the Grace of God, Go I

Each morning on the way to work,

I pass a man sitting in a cardboard box with plastic over it.

Legs sticking out!

Winter – cold.

Shoes – with holes – where scraps of newspaper instead of toes, stick out.

A small can sits in front next to a scribbled cardboard sign

.

Thank you – Praise the Lord.

This morning as I am about to pass the man and reach into my pocket for some change, the gentle snow flakes stop and the sky brightens just as I was murmuring to myself, *" There, but for the grace of God, go I."* I am overwhelmed with the reality of that phrase and its deepest meaning. What if I was that man and not vice president of… at that moment …I am compelled to bend down, take off my shoes and exchange them for his, as I do this, I hear a melodious

"There, but for the grace of God, go I "

I realize that I am cold – very cold – with frozen toes. I look up and I see a man in a warm elegant overcoat bending down and putting several coins in my box.

With frozen lips I say,

"Thank you - Praise the Lord."

OMG! When? How?

I entered the diner
Sat down
Looked at the menu,
And left

I picked up a paper
Looked at the headlines
Put it back on the rack,
And left

I got in the car
Drove to the lake.
Looked at the moon,
And left.

I grabbed my camera
Spotted a bird
Put lens cap on,
And left

Went to a bar

"What'll you have"

Looked at the options,

And left.

I called Siegfried

    The phone rang

        The phone rang

        The phone rang

Automated voice announcing:

"This phone has been permanently disconnected"

MARILYN RABETZ

MARILYN RABETZ is both an exhibiting color pencil artist, and a graphic designer with over 30 books published. One of her books, *Object Lessons, How to Draw Absolutely Anything*, is based on the drawing curriculum she created at The Loomis Chaffee School in Windsor, Connecticut, where she was an instructor of drawing, graphics and sculpture, and the Director of both the Richmond Art Center and the Visiting Artists Program. In addition she and her husband, Walter were the Directors of the Mercy Gallery. Her most recent book, *Marilyn Rabetz*, presents many of her paintings, each of which is paired with a writen discussion of its history, methodology and meaning.

Other Selections from QTR BOOKS

available at Amazon.com

- *Leaves,* photographs by Walter Rabetz, designed by Marilyn Rabetz

- *Marilyn Rabetz, Color Pencil Paintings by Marilyn Rabetz,* written and designed by Marilyn Rabetz

- *Home Room,Lew Wallace Jujior High School,*photographs by Walter Rabetz, designed by Marilyn Rabetz

- *Winters with the Pelicans, A basketball Memoir,* photos by Walter Rabetz, text by Marilyn and Walter Rabetz and designed by Marilyn Rabetz

- *Beauty at the Margins,* photographs by Walter Rabetz, designed by Marilyn Rabetz

- *Object Lessons, How to Draw Absolutely Anything,* written, illustrated, and designed by Marilyn Rabetz

- *Old Friends,* photographs by Walter Rabetz, designed by Marilyn Rabetz

- *The Agora, The Peekskill Coffee Shop,* photographs by Walter Rabetz, designed by Marilyn Rabetz

- *Summer Reading,* photographs by Walter Rabetz, designed by Marilyn Rabetz

- *Peekskill,* photographs by Walter Rabetz, designed by Marilyn Rabetz

- *The Bear Mountain Bridge,The Jewel of the Hudson,* photographs by Walter Rabetz, designed by Marilyn Rabetz

- *Dogway, The Walkway Over the Hudson River,* photographs by Walter Rabetz, designed by Marilyn Rabetz

- *The Ocean's Handwriting,* photographs by Walter Rabetz, designed by Marilyn Rabetz

- *A Fist Full of Stars,* poems by Dominic Failla, photographs by Walter Rabetz, designed by Marilyn Rabetz

- *Connecticut Fiddlers,* photographs by Siegfried Halus, designed by Marilyn Rabetz

- *Josiah Freeman, Nantucket Photographer, Late 19th Century Glass Plate Photographs by a Nantuicket Studio Photographer,* printed by Walter Rabetz, designed by Marilyn Rabetz

Made in the USA
Middletown, DE
28 March 2019